AN EASY-READ FACT BOOK

Space Shuttle

Michael Jay

Franklin Watts
London   New York   Toronto   Sydney

© 1984 Franklin Watts Ltd

First published in Great Britain
  1984 by
Franklin Watts Ltd
12a Golden Square
London W1

First published in the USA by
Franklin Watts Inc.
387 Park Avenue South
New York
N.Y. 10016

UK ISBN: 0 86313 077 1
US ISBN: 0-531-04708-3
Library of Congress Catalog Card
  Number: 83-50594

Photographs supplied by
Hewlett-Packard Ltd
NASA
Space Frontiers Ltd

Illustrated by
Christopher Forsey
Hayward Art Group
Hayward and Martin
Michael Roffe

Designed and produced by
David Jefferis

Technical consultant
Douglas Arnold of
  Space Frontiers Ltd

Printed in Great Britain by
  Cambus Litho, East Kilbride

AN EASY-READ FACT BOOK

Space Shuttle

Contents

The Shuttle system

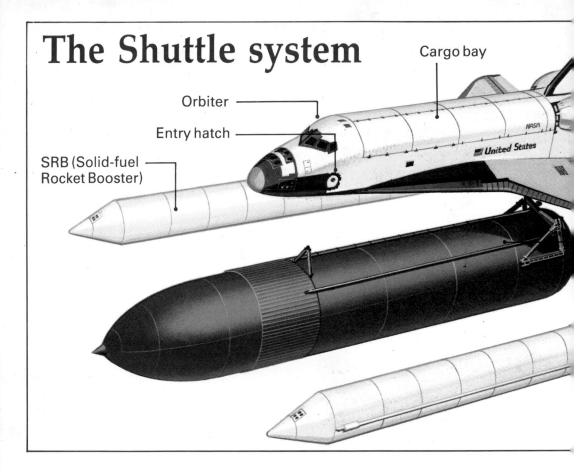

Cargo bay

Orbiter

Entry hatch

SRB (Solid-fuel
Rocket Booster)

NASA

United States

△Here you see the main parts of the Shuttle system – Orbiter, SRBs and the huge External Tank. Four Orbiters are planned at present – *Columbia*, *Challenger*, *Discovery* and *Atlantis*.

The Space Shuttle is the first spacecraft that can be used again and again.

The Shuttle Orbiter carries crew and cargo into space. It has wings and glides back to Earth, where it lands on a runway.

The giant External Tank (ET) holds liquid oxygen and liquid hydrogen. At take-off these fuels are pumped into the

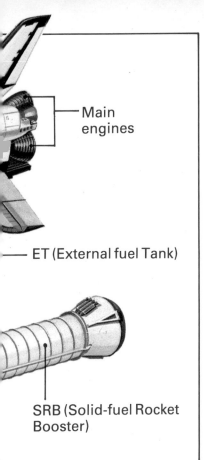

Main engines

ET (External fuel Tank)

SRB (Solid-fuel Rocket Booster)

Orbiter's three main engines. When the fuel is burned up, the ET is dropped into the ocean.

△ This model was used in early tests to check the shape of the Orbiter.

The two Solid-fuel Rocket Boosters (SRBs) use solid fuel. They work much like firework rockets. When empty, they parachute down to the sea. Unlike the ET, they can be refilled with fuel and used on another flight.

How the Shuttle works

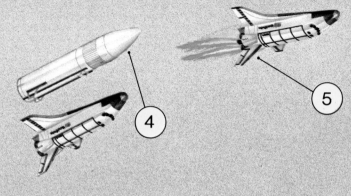

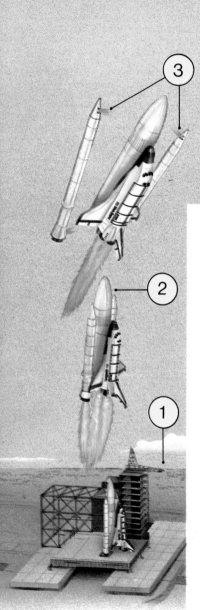

Here you can see a Shuttle from take-off to landing. Its trip takes it into orbit, where it circles on a path around the Earth.

A Shuttle is launched about every two months (1). A normal mission lasts for about a week. At lift-off, the two SRBs and three Orbiter main engines all burn together (2). When empty, the two SRBs drop away (3). Orbiter and ET fly on until the ET is empty. The tank is then dropped (4). The final "push" into space is given by two Orbital Maneuvering System (OMS) engines (5).

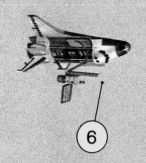

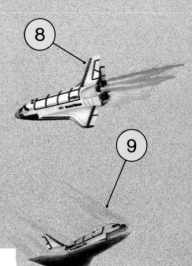

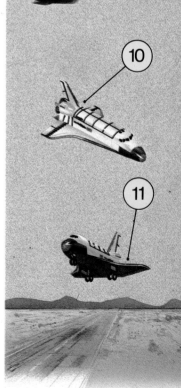

Once the Orbiter is circling the Earth, the cargo bay doors are opened (6). Perhaps the load is a laboratory or satellite (7). When it is time to return to Earth, the OMS engines are fired forward. This works like a brake, slowing the craft down (8). The Orbiter hits the upper atmosphere at about 16,465 mph (26,500 km/h), and parts of it glow red-hot with the heat of air friction (9).

The Orbiter glides toward the Earth (10), and its wheels are lowered just above the runway (11). After touchdown at 215 mph (346 km/h), the Orbiter rolls to a halt.

At the controls

△Astronauts John Young and Robert Crippen give the thumbs-up "OK" sign. Here they are practicing for the first Shuttle flight in the Orbiter *Columbia.* The successful flight began on April 12 1981.

The cockpit of the Orbiter looks much the same as that of a jet airliner. But there is one big difference. At take-off, the crew of the Shuttle lie on their backs, facing upwards into the sky.

At the controls is the commander, who is in charge of the flight. He sits on the left, with the pilot on the right. Groups of instruments face them, including several TV screens which display information about the ship's

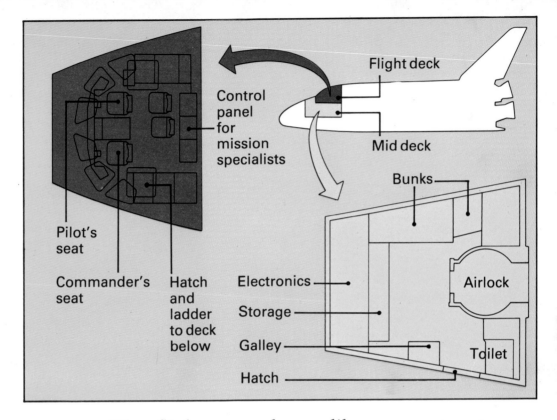

Pilot's seat

Commander's seat

Control panel for mission specialists

Hatch and ladder to deck below

Flight deck

Mid deck

Bunks

Electronics

Storage

Galley

Hatch

Airlock

Toilet

systems. The flight controls are like those of an aircraft. Foot pedals work the rudder. Pistol-grip controls pitch the nose up or down and roll the craft from side to side. In space, these controls are linked to groups of small gas jets that gently move the craft about.

There are two decks in the Orbiter. The flight deck is on the top level. Down below are the living quarters, airlock and hatch.

△ These plans show how the two decks on the Orbiter are arranged. Mission specialists – scientists who control various experiments – sit behind the pilot and commander. When the crew is big enough, more can sit in the mid-deck area.

Flight into orbit

On a Shuttle mission the crew board the Orbiter about two hours before lift-off. The time passes quickly, as many checks have first to be made. Then the countdown reaches zero!

SRBs and main engines roar together as the Shuttle clears the launch pad. The SRBs burn out 123 seconds later, and are dropped.

The craft flies faster, until it is 72 miles (116 km) up. Then the main engines shut off and the empty ET is dropped.

After two OMS thrusts, the Orbiter reaches its working height and speed. It is 45 minutes after lift-off and the craft is now 185 miles (298 km) up, traveling at 17,270 mph (27,800 km/h).

For the week of the mission, the crew live in zero-gravity. Without gravity, things are weightless. In orbital flight, things float around, with no "up" or "down."

▷Here you see *Columbia* thundering off the launch pad on its second mission.
    Women astronauts have traveled on later flights. Shuttle mission 7 included Sally Ride, America's first woman in space.

Living in space

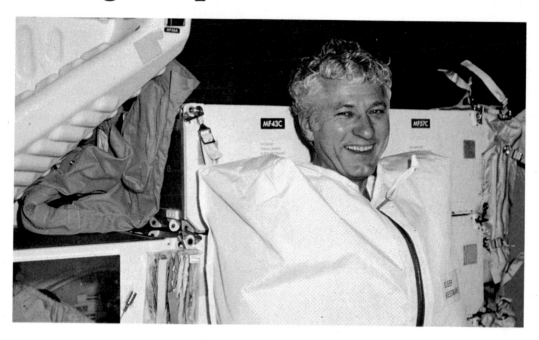

△Here, astronaut Henry Hartsfield shows how his sleep restraint bag works. Arms and legs are kept inside the bag to stop them from floating about in zero-gravity.

The Orbiter is planned to keep the men and women aboard as safe and comfortable as possible. The craft has to be a "mini-Earth." It carries all that is necessary for life, for in space there is no air, water or food.

The air supply is made up of nitrogen and oxygen, much like the gases we breathe on Earth. Carbon dioxide, the poison waste gas we breathe out, is absorbed by special canisters of lithium hydroxide.

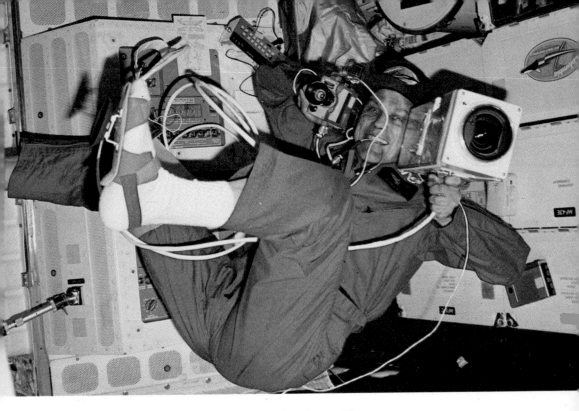

Electricity is made by fuel cells, which also supply about 7 lb (3 kg) of water every hour. This water is pure, so it can be used for both drinking and washing.

Food is stored in the ship's galley. Some comes ready mixed in foil pouches. Water needs to be added to other foods. The evening meal might include shrimp cocktail, beef steak and butterscotch pudding, washed down with tasty grape juice.

△ Ken Mattingly shows off movie and TV cameras. Suction cups on his sandals keep him stuck firmly to the Orbiter's deck when he is working at an instrument panel.

Both this picture and the one opposite were taken on the fourth Shuttle mission.

Science in orbit

The Space Shuttle's huge cargo bay is just right for carrying big satellite loads into space. The same cargo bay is used to hold Spacelab, a cylindrical space laboratory. Scientists can float to and from the Orbiter living sections, entering Spacelab through an airlock tube at one end. Inside the laboratory, scientists can work in the comfort of air-conditioning. Much of their experiment equipment is mounted outside Spacelab, on steel pallets.

▷ This is one of two communications satellites taken up on the fifth Shuttle mission. The satellite, with its booster rocket, was stored in a container, to protect it from harm during launch.

▽ This picture shows the European Spacelab, a laboratory in which scientists can work without spacesuits.

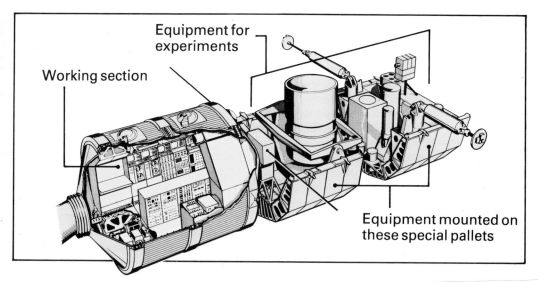

Working section

Equipment for experiments

Equipment mounted on these special pallets

Spacewalking

▽ Shuttle spacesuits are made in several sizes – astronauts alter straps inside for a perfect fit. Once switched on, the suit has air and power for seven hours, plus an emergency 30-minute air-supply. Two suits are usually carried aboard each Orbiter.

The Shuttle spacesuit is much better than earlier designs, and is cheaper. The arms and legs bend more easily and the suit is easier to put on. Early astronauts took a long time to struggle into their spacesuits, even with the help of fellow crew members.

Another Shuttle "first" is the Manned Maneuvering Unit (MMU). This is a big backpack, stored in the cargo

Cooling garment

Lower body and legs

Upper body and arms

Joined up round the waist

Gloves on

◁ The first Shuttle spacewalk was from the *Challenger* on Mission 6. Here you can see mission specialists Story Musgrave (left) and Donald Peterson floating around the ship's cargo bay. No MMU was used on this mission.

bay. It allows an astronaut to move freely in space or to another spacecraft. It has 24 nozzles which squirt jets of nitrogen gas to push the MMU about.

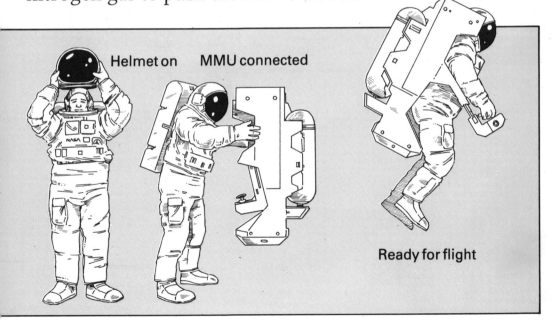

Helmet on   MMU connected

Ready for flight

Many different missions

The Orbiter fleet will carry a wide range of equipment into space.

Cargoes will include comsats and telescopes. Comsats beam TV, radio and television signals from one side of the world to the other. Telescopes include the powerful Space Telescope, which will look seven times further into space than any telescope down on Earth. It should also be able to find objects 50 times fainter than now possible. It might even spot planets circling other stars.

Military loads on board the Shuttle are kept secret, but most military satellites carry powerful cameras. These are used to check the missile bases, airfields and naval equipment of various countries.

In the late 1980s we could see the Shuttle being used to supply manned space stations and orbital laboratories, far bigger than Spacelab.

△ Large space stations of the future may be built by the Grumman beam builder. The beam builder is a robot, able to make lightweight metal girders in space.

▷ Boeing Aerospace thought of this idea for using empty fuel tanks to build up a large manned Space Operations Center.

Fiery re-entry

△ To return to Earth, Orbiters fire twin rocket motors to slow down.

To return from space, the Orbiter swings round to face backwards. The OMS engines are fired for 2½ minutes to slow it down. The Orbiter is then swung nose-forward again and, slowed by the OMS burn, gradually loses height.

At about 50 miles (80 km) up, the Orbiter plummets through the upper atmosphere, glowing with the heat of air friction. A layer of special tiles and insulation absorbs this heat, of up to 3,000°F (1,648°C). Sitting in the cabin, the crew can see a pink glow outside the cockpit window. This is the super-heated air passing by at high speed.

The heat affects radio, and all contact with ground control is lost. But after 12 minutes, the Orbiter has slowed to 8,275 mph (13,317 km/h). The radio starts working again and the all-clear is given to land on the runway, now just twelve minutes away.

△ During re-entry
through the Earth's
atmosphere, parts of the
Orbiter reach very hot
temperatures.

▷ This computer view
shows scientists how
the Orbiter's frame will
heat up during re-entry.
The hottest parts appear
white, the coolest are
purple.

Runway touchdown

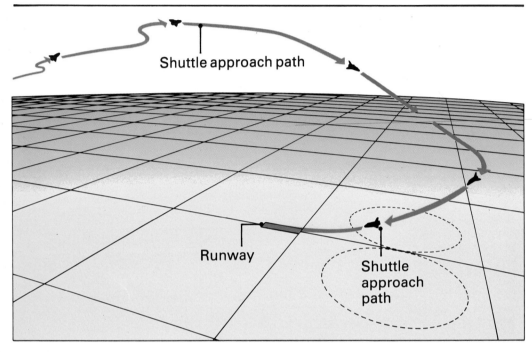

Shuttle approach path

Runway

Shuttle approach path

△ Orbiters glide down without rocket power, so every landing has to be exactly right. The wheels are lowered just 14 seconds before touchdown.

Final touchdown is computer-controlled, although the Orbiter can be flown by the crew if necessary. The craft drops rapidly and glides toward the runway. Several chase planes stationed near by follow the Orbiter down. Cameras and pilots check every second of the approach.

Just 90 ft (27 m) above the ground, the landing gear is lowered. Then the nose pitches up, and the Orbiter

settles on to the runway at 215 mph (346 km/h). Speedbrakes pop out from the tailfin, the craft rolls to a halt and the mission is nearly over.

All that is left is to check and switch off various systems. Ground crews drive up in trucks to take charge and the astronauts are free to leave the craft through the hatch.

The Orbiter will now be taken away to be prepared for its next flight.

△ After the landing, ground crews empty fuel tanks and check for leaks or spillages which might cause a fire.

Emergency!

△ In an emergency on the launch pad, astronauts climb from the Orbiter's hatch into two-man steel baskets. The five baskets slide down wires to a concrete bunker 1,200 ft (366 m) away. The long slide takes 35 seconds.

Something could go wrong on any mission, so Shuttle designers have added many safety features.

If fire breaks out on the launch pad, a slide wire escape system can be used. Astronauts jump into steel baskets attached to the service tower. The baskets slide down long steel cables to an underground bunker.

The Orbiter has smoke detectors and fire extinguishers to guard against fire

outbreaks, on the ground or in space.

If the order to "abandon ship" happens in space, two astronauts can wear spacesuits. Any other people on board are carried in fabric "rescue balls."

Each Orbiter carries a medical kit, which is enough to cope with most injuries or illness. Most astronauts suffer from space-sickness, so medicine for this must be carried on any space mission.

△ For space rescues, astronauts have to be zipped into rescue balls 34 in (86 cm) wide. A spacesuited crewmate carries the ball to a nearby rescue ship. Each ball has oxygen for 20 minutes and a small porthole.

Future-shuttle

The present Orbiter fleet should last for many years, but already planners have thought of ideas for new and improved versions. These include bigger fuel tanks, passenger pods and Shuttles with cargo only.

The craft shown on these pages is a mini-Shuttle, to be launched from the back of a Boeing 747 jetliner. The 747 would have a rocket motor mounted in its tail to push it higher and faster than a

normal plane. At 37,000 ft (11,278 m) the mini-Shuttle would break free of the 747 and fly up into orbit, using a supply of fuel stored in its big underbelly tank.

Like the Shuttle of today, the small craft would glide down to land on a runway. The mini-Shuttle would be very useful, as the "launch pad" could be any runway long enough to allow a 747 to take off.

△ This possible mini-Shuttle of the 1990s has just taken off from its 747 carrier plane. Like the Shuttle of today, the "mini" drops its fuel tank when it is empty.

Facts and figures

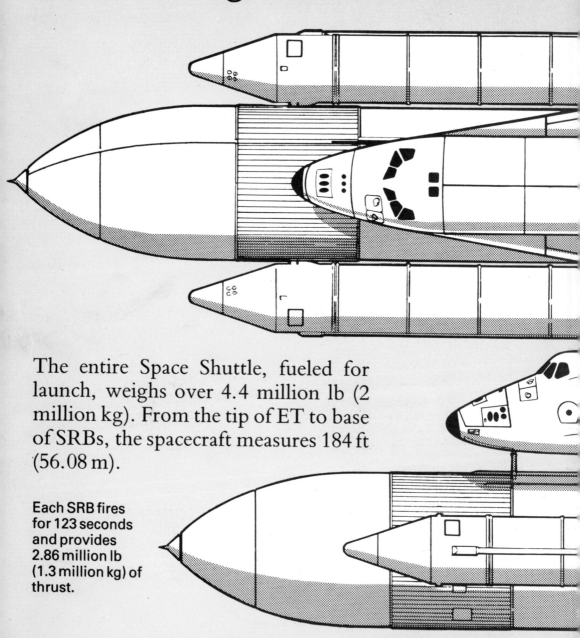

The entire Space Shuttle, fueled for launch, weighs over 4.4 million lb (2 million kg). From the tip of ET to base of SRBs, the spacecraft measures 184 ft (56.08 m).

Each SRB fires for 123 seconds and provides 2.86 million lb (1.3 million kg) of thrust.

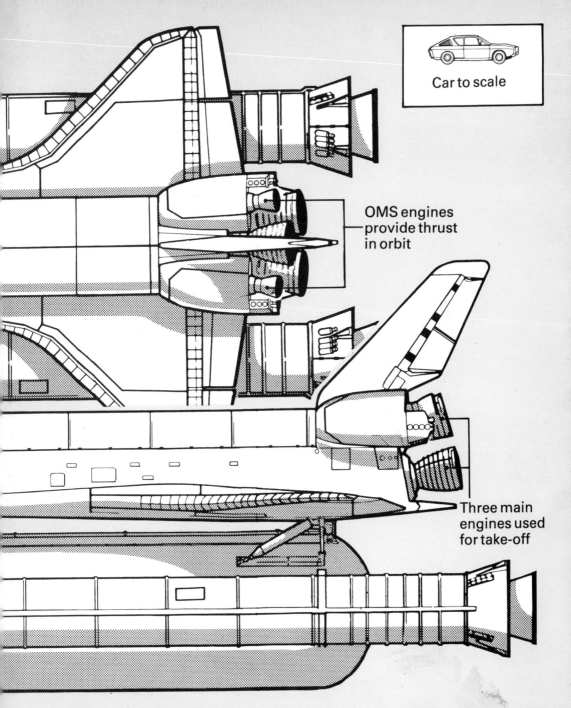

Car to scale

OMS engines
provide thrust
in orbit

Three main
engines used
for take-off

29

Facts and figures *continued*

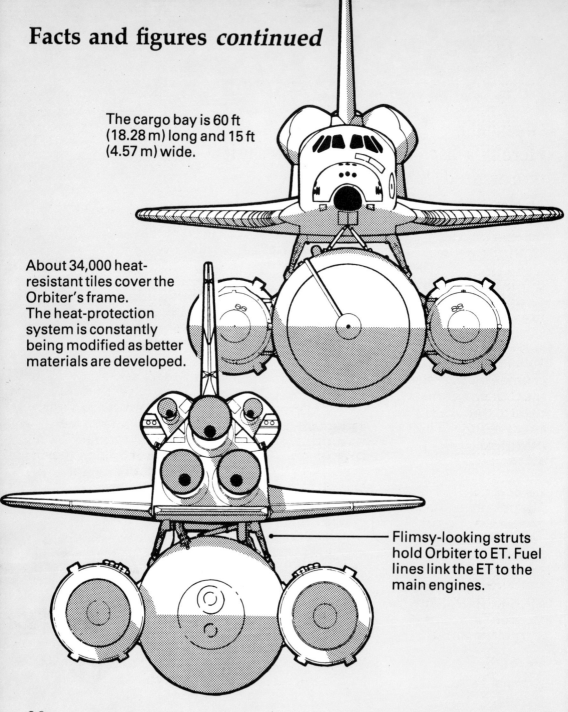

The cargo bay is 60 ft (18.28 m) long and 15 ft (4.57 m) wide.

About 34,000 heat-resistant tiles cover the Orbiter's frame. The heat-protection system is constantly being modified as better materials are developed.

Flimsy-looking struts hold Orbiter to ET. Fuel lines link the ET to the main engines.

Glossary

Here is a list of some of the technical words used in this book.

Air friction
The rubbing effect of moving air, which causes heat. The Orbiter's speed as it re-enters the atmosphere causes parts of the craft to glow with heat.

Airlock
Two-door man-sized chamber carried aboard the Orbiter. Astronauts use it to climb out into space without letting air out of Orbiter living areas.

Carbon dioxide
The poisonous waste gas we breathe out.

Comsat
Communications satellite. A comsat is any satellite which sends radio or TV signals around the world.

ET
External Tank.

Fuel cell
Device which mixes oxygen and hydrogen to make electricity and water.

Lithium hydroxide
Chemical used to absorb carbon dioxide from the Orbiter's air system.

MMU
Manned Maneuvering Unit. The backpack astronauts use to move about in space near the Orbiter.

Mission specialist
Crew member, in charge of satellite launches and who sees that the mission's scientific aims are carried out.
   Also, payload specialists can be carried. They are scientists in charge of particular experiments. *All* people in an Orbiter share the housework!

Orbit
Path in which a smaller object repeatedly travels around a larger one. A Shuttle Orbiter passes around the Earth every 90 minutes. The Earth orbits the Sun once a year.

OMS
Orbital Maneuvering System.

Re-entry
Returning to the Earth's atmosphere from space.

SRB
Solid-fuel Rocket Booster.

Speedbrakes
The Orbiter's rudder splits into two sections, pushing out into the airflow. In the final stages of landing, they help slow the craft down.

Service tower
Metal structure which lets the ground crew get to parts of the Shuttle before a launch. The Shuttle takes off from a mobile launch platform, which is taken to the launch area on a huge caterpillar-track crawler vehicle.

31

Index